# THE MERCHANT OF VENICE

Cover Design by Nancy Peach

High Noon Books
*A division of Academic Therapy Publications*
20 Commercial Boulevard
Novato, CA 94949-6191

International Standard Book Number: 1-57128-123-1

9 8 7 6
1 0 9 8 7 6 5 4

Another attractive book in the Streamlined Shakespeare series is *Romeo and Juliet*. Write for a free list of High Noon Books titles.

# Table of Contents

# ABOUT
# WILLIAM SHAKESPEARE
## (1564-1616)

William Shakespeare was born in Stratford-on-Avon, a market town about eighty miles northwest of London. His father was a glovemaker and a trader in wool, hides, and grain. The family, which had eight children, while not rich, led a comfortable life. William was the third child in the family, and it is thought that he attended the Stratford grammar school where classes started at six or seven in the morning and lasted until five or six in the late afternoon. When the family's finances declined, it became necessary for him to leave school to go to work for a local tradesman.

He married Anne Hathaway when he was eighteen and she was twenty-six. They had three children, including twins.

It is not known exactly when or why Shakespeare left Stratford and moved to London where he quickly became involved in the theater both as an actor and a playwright. Theaters in London were closed from 1592 to 1594 because of the terrifying plague that swept throughout Europe, so Shakespeare spent his time writing plays and publishing two long narrative poems that immediately became popular and started him on the road to fame.

We can tell from the records of the number of properties he bought in London and Stratford that his income was more than ample. His days were busy acting at the Blackfriar and Globe Theaters and writing new plays to be performed there.

Shakespeare was only 52 when he died in Stratford. His birthplace and Anne Hathaway's cottage have been furnished to look as much as possible as they did in Shakespeare's time and are visited by thousands of tourists and admirers each year.

To this day Shakespeare's works can be found on stages in every country in the world. The work of no other playwright has been performed in so many nations throughout so many centuries. His friend Ben Johnson wrote in 1623, "He was not of an age, but for all of time." By now we know Johnson's observation was absolutely correct!

# THE MERCHANT OF VENICE

## THE STORY

# Part I

I have a story to tell. It is a story of love and hatred. A story of generosity and greed. A story of fortune and misfortune. A story of laughter and tears. It is a story about strength of character and quick thinking. Though this story was told long ago, its message has as much meaning today as it did then.

The events happened in a beautiful city in Italy. This city, Venice, rests like a crown jewel on the Adriatic Sea. A money lender named Shylock lived here. He had made a fortune by lending money to merchants. He was known as a hard-hearted man because of the way he forced borrowers to repay him. Very few people liked Shylock. Some people didn't like him because of the way he ran his loan business. Others did not like him because he was Jewish. At that time there was a lot of bad feeling between Christians and Jews.

Of all the merchants in Venice, there was one who especially hated Shylock. This merchant's name was Antonio. Shylock returned the hatred. He despised the way Antonio lent money to people who were in trouble but did not charge them interest. These loans took business away from Shylock.

Antonio and Shylock often ran into one another at the Rialto. This was the business center of the town. When the two met, they would have arguments. Sometimes these arguments were about religion. Other times they were over business. Antonio would scold Shylock for being such a heartless money lender. It may have seemed that Shylock was patiently listening to Antonio. But he wasn't. He was really plotting ways to get even with him.

Antonio was much admired by most of his fellow citizens – except Shylock. He was thought to be one of the kindest men in Venice. His fellow merchants talked about him with deep respect. They felt that he was a symbol of all that was good and honest. They knew that they could count on him in hard times.

Antonio's best friend was a young man whose name was Bassanio. Bassanio was born to a wealthy family. He was known as a noble Venetian gentleman. Even though his parents were rich, he had little money himself. His family had given him a fortune. He had wasted it on lavish living. He did not plan ahead for the future. This was very common for young men during this time. Their parents did not teach them the importance of careful spending. As a result, many of them had money problems.

Bassanio had come up against money troubles in the past. He had turned to Antonio for help many times before. In fact, he already owed a good sum of money to him. Antonio had always been generous. He treated Bassanio like a brother. He was happy to share his money with his friend. Antonio told Bassanio, "My money is your money."

One day Bassanio came to Antonio for another loan. This time Bassanio had fallen in love. The woman he loved was named Portia. She was heir to a large fortune. Her wealthy father had died. And she had recently inherited his money. Here was a beautiful woman whom he dearly loved, who also happened to be rich. Bassanio described her to Antonio. She was the loveliest woman he had ever seen. He could think of nothing else but making her his wife.

Bassanio thought that Portia returned his love. He had visited her house several times before her father died. Each time he was there, he caught her looking at him in certain ways. He felt that her eyes were saying that she cared for him. Bassanio thought that if he could just buy some new clothes and gifts for Portia, he might win her. Unfortunately, he had no money – not even enough for food that week.

Bassanio had only one way to get money – Antonio. However, this was not a good time for him to be asking for money. Antonio was broke. It was the end of the month. He had already spent all of his cash on goods that were soon to arrive by ship. Antonio did have an idea though.

"Bassanio," said Antonio, "I think I know how we can solve your problem. I know a money lender who always has cash on hand. His name is Shylock. We'll go to him and ask for a loan. He is certain to lend you money if I sign the loan agreement. I expect several of my ships to dock any day now. As soon as these ships come in, we'll pay him back from the money we make on the goods."

Bassanio was happy. He knew Antonio would help him. What a great friend! The two went to the Rialto to find Shylock.

# Part II

While Antonio and Bassanio were looking for Shylock, Portia was facing her own problems. Bassanio didn't know it, but proposing to Portia was going to be difficult. Her wealthy father had arranged the conditions of her marriage before he died. He did not want her to choose her own husband. He was afraid that she would make a poor choice. He wanted to be sure that she married a man who was worthy of her. He made a plan for selecting a worthy suitor.

Before he died, Portia's father set up three chests in a room. One chest was gold, one silver, and one lead. In one of these chests was a small portrait of Portia. If the suitor chose the right box, he would find the picture of Portia. Finding this picture meant that the man could then propose to her. Portia's father felt that the best husband would know which box to choose.

If the man failed to pick the right box, he would have to leave the house right away. He could never court Portia or any other woman for the rest of his life. Every man who failed to win Portia would never be able to marry, or even have a girlfriend. Each man had to swear to these terms before he could go into the room with the three chests. It was a big risk. But Portia's father felt that the chance of winning his daughter should be worth such a risk.

Portia was tired of having men come through her house. She was a bright woman. She was unhappy that her father didn't trust her to choose a husband. Her good friend and servant, Nerissa, tried to convince her that her father had done the right thing. Nerissa believed that a good husband could be found this way. Portia was not so sure. She complained that these men were dull. They had poor manners and were vain. Many had bad habits, such as drinking too much.

Portia was different from most women of that time. She had a mind of her own. She didn't want others to make decisions for her. Most women accepted the fact that their families would arrange their marriages. Portia believed that she was as smart, or smarter, than any man. It made Portia sad to think that she was probably going to end up with a boring husband with bad habits.

Portia did not like any of the men who had come to court her so far. She told Nerissa, "There's not one who is decent. They are all deadly dull or impossible. I guess I should feel lucky that most of them have been scared off by my father's terms."

"Portia," said Nerissa, "do you remember a man from Venice? A man who was a scholar and a soldier?"

Portia's eyes started to sparkle. She had never forgotten this man. She had thought many times of his handsome face and gentle ways. He seemed to be a charming person who was also caring, kind, and intelligent. She tried not to think too much about him. She felt it was hopeless. She was a woman who could not choose a husband. She could do little but wait for some man to choose her.

"Yes, I remember him. How could I forget? His name is Bassanio. Let's not talk about him. It just makes me feel sad," Portia said.

At that time, a servant entered the room. He said, "Madam, a messenger for the Prince of Morocco has just arrived. The Prince will be arriving this evening."

"Oh, that's just wonderful," said Portia. "Another unsuitable suitor. I wonder what problems this one will have.

Meanwhile in Venice, Antonio and Bassanio had found Shylock. He was at the Rialto just as they thought he would be.

"Shylock, I have a request for you. I would like you to lend my best friend, Bassanio, three thousand ducats. I'll be glad to co-sign the loan papers with him. You can count on me to pay any interest you require." Antonio explained that this money would be repaid from the goods on the ships that would be docking shortly.

Bassanio chimed in, "You can be sure that I'm good for this loan. I will pay you back. However, Antonio's name should be enough for you." The truth of the matter was that nearly everyone in Venice knew that Bassanio had big debts. It's a good thing that he had a friend like Antonio.

"Let's go out to dinner and talk more about this loan," said Bassanio.

Shylock answered, "I never eat with Christians. I may walk with them, lend them money, but I won't eat with them. Not ever. I don't want to sit there and smell pork. It turns my stomach to think about it."

"Very well," said Bassanio, "just give me the loan that I ask for. What about it?"

Shylock could hardly believe his ears. What foolish men these were! Although he was listening to the words of Antonio and Bassanio, he was thinking about other things. How many times had Antonio scolded him in front of the other merchants of Venice? He had complained about Shylock's high interest rates in a loud angry voice that everyone could hear. He also said nasty things about Shylock's religion. Antonio acted as if he were better because his religion was Christianity.

Antonio's past words were easily remembered because they had bothered him so. Shylock was thinking about how he might finally be able to get even with Antonio. He heard Antonio shout, "Shylock, are you going to give us the money or not?"

Shylock slowly began his answer. "Antonio, do you recall all those times that you insulted me? Do you remember spitting on my clothes and calling me a dog? Now you want to borrow money from a dog! Does a dog have money? Go find one with three thousand ducats. You insulted me and then you ask me for a loan."

"Just because I ask you for a loan doesn't mean I have changed my mind about you," said Antonio. "I still think you are a dog. I look forward to spitting on you again in the future. I'm not asking you for a favor. You are no friend of mine. Make no mistake about that. I'm asking you for a loan. If I don't pay you back, you can place a heavy fine on me." He knew his ships would be in soon.

"Antonio, you don't have to be so angry," said Shylock in a low soft voice. "I would like nothing better than to be friends with you. I am willing to let bygones be bygones. I will give you the money. I'm not even going to charge you interest for the loan."

Antonio couldn't believe his ears. "What did you say?"

"My friend, I said you have misjudged me. I am not the heartless person that you think. You are in need of help. I am here to assist you. I'm going to give you three thousand ducats without any interest. How's that for a deal, my dear boy? Three thousand ducats interest free."

"Is it possible that I may have judged you too harshly?" asked Antonio.

"I think you have," said Shylock. "I am happy to lend you this money. This money is a loan that bears no

16

interest. I want only your respect and gratitude. Let me see. How could we seal this bargain? Yes, I have it!"

"How shall we seal this agreement?" asked Antonio.

"Come with me and see a lawyer. Sign an agreement saying this is an interest-free loan. But if you don't pay it back, you will give me a pound of your flesh. From any part of your body that I choose! This will be a great joke for the other merchants to talk about for years to come. No one will ever believe this loan arrangement!"

"A pound of flesh!" cringed Bassanio. "That's not even funny."

Antonio was also taken aback. He was silent for a few moments. Antonio liked a joke as well as the next person. Shylock had really been a good sport about this loan. Antonio thought that signing the loan agreement was the least he could do for this favor. Just think! No interest for such a huge loan! He was surprised and pleased that Shylock had turned out to have a heart and a sense of humor. Yet, he didn't really think that the idea of taking a pound of flesh was very funny. In fact, it was a joke in poor taste. But since he was getting the money for his friend, he put up with Shylock's bad taste.

"Shylock, I will be happy to sign your loan agreement in front of a lawyer. And may I say that I am touched by your kindness," Antonio said. He decided not to say anything about the pound of flesh.

Bassanio was starting to feel uncomfortable about this loan. Something just didn't feel right. He would have preferred to pay interest. The condition of the pound of flesh bothered him. Although he knew that Shylock could not possibly be serious about such a penalty, he still didn't like this kind of joke. He pulled Antonio aside. He said, "Antonio, don't sign any paper with those terms. I don't trust this man. Let's just walk away. We'll figure something else out."

17

"No, I won't hear of it. You're going to get your money, your fancy clothes, and your wife! This fellow just wants a good laugh. After all, it's only fair. I've made him feel bad many times. This is his way of forgiving and forgetting. Besides, the ships with the cargo are as good as in the dock now. Quit worrying! Nothing can go wrong," said Antonio.

"Antonio, I have a bad feeling about this," said Bassanio. He was interrupted by Shylock.

"You Christians do not trust people. Is that how your religion teaches you to live? Listen here, Bassanio. What could I possibly have to gain by taking a pound of flesh from your friend? Why would I do such a thing? A pound of beef or a pound of lamb would be another thing. There isn't any risk to signing the agreement. It's my way of saying that past bad feelings between us are finished. Let's start over and be friends. An interest-free loan and a bond of friendship. That is what I offer. I don't know what else to do, but say good-bye to you. I wish you better luck with another money lender." With that, Shylock turned to go.

"Wait, Shylock," said Antonio. "My friend is too careful. He's like an old lady. I'll sign your loan papers. I thank you for this chance. Let's get on with the closing so my good friend can get on with his life!"

A strange smile came over Shylock's face. He grinned from ear to ear. Yet, it was not exactly a happy smile. There was some other feeling behind the smile. Antonio didn't seem to notice.

Shylock was enjoying himself at this moment. He didn't realize that something very important was happening at the same time. Something that would soon upset him.

# Part III

Shylock had a beautiful daughter named Jessica. While Antonio and Bassanio were sealing the loan agreement, Jessica was making plans. She was planning to run away from her father. She was going to marry Lorenzo, a Christian. Jessica had also made up her mind to change religions. She wanted to be a Christian like her groom. This would upset her father more than anything she had ever done.

Although Bassanio still had a bad feeling about this loan arrangement, he found it hard to be unhappy. He took the money that Antonio had borrowed. He bought all the fine clothes and gifts that he needed to propose to Portia. She lived close by Venice in Belmont, a smaller town. Once he had loaded the gifts, he and his servant, Gratiano, were ready for the trip.

Luckily, Bassanio had been right. It was true. Portia had been sending him unspoken messages of love when he had visited her before. She was in love with him. She had been secretly hoping that he returned this feeling. Portia had been waiting such a long time for him to return. She could scarcely believe her happiness when Bassanio arrived at her home. It meant that there was a chance her dream could come true.

When Bassanio confessed to Portia that he was without money, she did not care. Since Bassanio was born into a wealthy family, he could offer her a respected name but little else. Portia had no interest in Bassanio's money.

This was very unusual at the time. Most rich young women would not have married someone without wealth. Portia was different. Money meant nothing to her. Since she had her own fortune, it was unnecessary that her husband be rich. If only he could choose the right chest, everything would be perfect.

Portia started to worry. She didn't want him to choose right away. What if he chose the wrong box? He would have to leave and never return.

"Bassanio, don't choose the box today," Portia softly said. "Wait a few days, please."

"Why should I wait? The sooner I choose, the sooner you will be my wife," said Bassanio.

"What if you choose the wrong box? I will lose you forever."

Bassanio was touched by her words. She truly cared for him! "Portia, I must choose now. This is like torture to me. I have to find out if I can be your husband."

"Please, I beg of you. Say that you will stay here with me for a few days. No, stay for a month. I will teach you how to choose the right chest. What am I saying? I can't do that. I promised my father," said Portia.

"Portia, I must choose now. I can't wait a minute longer."

Portia gave in. "All right. If you must, you must. First let me get a musician to play for you while you are choosing. This might help you." Portia called for her musician. He began to play a soft soothing melody.

Bassanio slowly walked over to the golden chest. He looked at it carefully. "This is not it," he said to himself. "It's just too obvious. Everyone would choose the gold on first thought. Not I. Portia's father was trying to separate good men from fools."

He moved on to the silver chest. "This is not it either. It would be the second most obvious choice." Then his eyes settled on the lead chest. "This is it! I feel it in my bones." He opened the chest slowly. He could not believe what he found. The tiny portrait of his love! Next to the picture was a rolled-up note. He read the words. They told him that he could turn to Portia and give her a loving kiss. She now belonged to him. He had won her hand!

Bassanio was beside himself with happiness. He turned to Portia and said, "I'm so happy. I can't find the words to tell you of my joy." Bassanio ran to kiss Portia.

Portia had been so nervous as she watched Bassanio make his choice. She hardly breathed as she watched him move from chest to chest. She thought her heart would stop beating. Now all of those feelings rushed to the surface. As he reached for her, Portia said, "Oh, Bassanio, I can't believe this. I am the luckiest woman in all of Italy."

Bassanio was humbled by his good fortune. He tried to tell her that he was not worthy of her. Portia would not listen to these words. She was the kind of woman that any man would have been lucky to marry. Instead of listening to Bassanio's words about his faults, she tried to make him feel as if he were better than she. Every time Bassanio would say something about *his* poverty or shortcomings, Portia would talk about *her* flaws.

"Portia, please, it is I who do not deserve you," answered Bassanio.

"Yesterday I was nothing," said Portia. "Just the mistress of this mansion, these servants, and these grounds. Today, I have the chance to give it all to you along with myself if you will have us. Please take this ring and show me that you will accept me and all I have. Promise me that you will never take it off."

Bassanio could not believe how lucky he was. She accepted him and his poverty with open arms. He took her ring and vowed he would wear it always. To his death. He made this promise to her.

This scene between Bassanio and Portia had been watched by others. Gratiano, Bassanio's servant, and Nerissa, Portia's servant, had been in the room during the choosing of the chest. They had both heard Portia consent to be Bassanio's wife. Gratiano now had a request of his own. He asked Bassanio if he also could be married. Bassanio was so happy at that moment, he would have agreed to almost anything. He was very pleased to give Gratiano permission to marry. He told him, "I would love to see you get married. I would like you to be as happy as I am now. I only hope that you can get someone to be your wife!"

Gratiano told him that he wanted to marry Nerissa. Both Bassanio and Portia were surprised. Gratiano explained that he and Nerissa had talked about marriage before. Nerissa had said that she would marry him only if Portia married Bassanio.

Portia asked, "Is this true, Nerissa?"

"Yes, it is true. You know I would only marry if you approve," she added.

Both Portia and Bassanio were delighted. The fact that their servants were also in love served to strengthen their own feelings. They seemed truly meant for one another. Bassanio said to the couple, "Your marriage is the best possible thing that could happen. We would be honored to have you married at our own wedding. It will be a double wedding!"

Alas! The happiness of the moment didn't last long. A messenger arrived at the door. The letter that he brought had terrible news. As Bassanio read the note, his face became white. He had to sit down before he fell. His hands were trembling. Portia thought that his best friend must have died. "What on earth is the matter?"

she cried.

"You will never believe this. This is the worst thing that could ever have happened," he said.

"What is it? Please tell me!" cried Portia. She could not stand to see her beloved in such a state.

"This is my fault, Portia. I haven't been completely honest with you. I told you that I was broke. I didn't tell you I was also in debt." Bassanio went on to tell her the story about Antonio and Shylock. This time he told her everything. He explained that it was his fault that Antonio had borrowed money from Shylock. Bassanio also told the part about the penalty for not repaying the money. He then read Antonio's letter.

*Dear Bassanio,*

*My ships are all lost. The unthinkable has happened. Shylock insists that the penalty be enforced. Everyone has tried to talk him out of it. Even the Duke of Venice has tried. He will listen to no one. Shylock wants a pound of my flesh. Who could have believed that this could happen? I am going to die. Please come to the trial and my execution. I want to see you one more time before I die. I will understand if you do not come. It is going to be a gruesome event.*

*Your friend, Antonio*

Portia was shocked at the words Bassanio read. How could this be? This money lender was going to cut a pound of flesh off another man's body? That could not possibly happen. Or could it? A chill ran through Portia's body. She felt cold to the bone. She recovered quickly. "Bassanio, go to your friend at once," she said. "I will give you enough money to repay this debt. I will give twenty times the original loan. Go at once before your best friend is harmed. You will never forgive yourself unless you save him."

Then Portia had another thought. "Before you go, we should be married. If you are my husband, you will legally have the right to all my money. You must use whatever you need to save Antonio."

The wedding was not as happy as they had planned. Bassanio and Portia were worried about Antonio. Even Gratiano and Nerissa's marriage did not make them feel better. Everyone felt their sadness.

As soon as the wedding was over, Bassanio left. He traveled as quickly as he could. Bassanio found his good friend in prison. He told Antonio that he would go to Shylock and repay the debt. Thanks to the wealth of his new wife and the greed of Shylock, he was sure he could free Antonio. Bassanio was so confident of the outcome that Antonio started to feel better.

The meeting with Shylock did not go well. Bassanio could not believe what he heard. Shylock told him that he would not accept repayment of the debt. He said that the date for repayment was past. Bassanio offered him double the original loan. The answer was no. He offered him triple the original loan. The answer was no. On his knees he begged Shylock to name any amount of money. Shylock said, "I want no money. I want the pound of flesh."

There was no way to solve this problem. It was sent to the court of Venice. The Duke of Venice was asked to be the judge in this shocking case. All of Venice was talking about it. They had never heard or seen anything like this in their town before. Bassanio was worried about the trial. He couldn't eat or sleep. He was so ashamed about his part in this. If only he had known what was going to happen. He could not forgive himself.

Portia could not understand. How could a man be so

evil that he would want to kill another over a debt? The truth of the matter was that there was more than money involved in this case. Shylock was an evil man. He wanted revenge for Antonio's treatment of him. But something else had also happened to make him crazy with anger. His only child, Jessica, had eloped with a Christian. When she left her home, she took a lot of money and a big diamond from her father's house. Not only did his daughter leave him for a Christian, but she had stolen from him, too. To make matters worse, she had married a man who was living in Bassanio's house. Shylock heard that she was going to give up her own religion and become a Christian. This was just too much for him to bear.

Shylock thought that Antonio and Bassanio were mixed up in this. He thought that they had encouraged Jessica to steal from him. He also thought that they had urged her to marry their friend. Shylock was in a rage by this turn of events. He was running all around Venice crying out, "My daughter, my money. I have lost my daughter and my money. What could be worse than this?" People who saw him thought he had lost his mind.

Portia did not know any of this so she could not understand what was happening. She only knew that something was very wrong here. When Portia said good-bye to Bassanio, she had been cheerful. She told him that everything would work out. Portia also said that Bassanio should bring Antonio home when he was released from prison. She spoke of having a party when they returned. In her heart, Portia did not think that things were going to go well. When Bassanio was gone, she didn't have to act cheerful about this situation. She sat down and began to think of all the things that could go wrong.

Portia was very clever. She thought about the

problem from every angle. She now felt that she had better develop a plan to save her husband's friend. She could not rely on fate to change the course of events. Portia knew she was needed in Venice.

She sat down at her desk. She began writing a letter to her cousin Bellario. He was a well-known lawyer. Portia explained Antonio's case to him. She asked for his opinion. She also asked to borrow the clothes he wore in court. At that time in Italy, all lawyers had to wear long robes, wigs, and large hats when they went to court. A messenger soon returned with Bellario's answer. The messenger brought a box with Bellario's court robes and a letter. In this letter were his instructions for defending Antonio.

Portia dressed herself in the court robes at once. She also made Nerissa dress in a court robe. Nerissa did not like this idea. But she could not refuse. Portia wanted Nerissa to play the role of the lawyer's clerk. They set off for Venice together and arrived on the day of the trial. They made their way to the Grand Court House of Venice. The case was to be heard before the Duke of Venice. The Grand Court House was the largest in the city. This case was well known. This court house was chosen so that many citizens could hear this unusual case.

# Part IV

When Portia entered the courtroom, she gave a letter to the Duke of Venice. He was to judge Antonio's case. The letter was from Bellario. It said that he could not represent Antonio in court because he was sick. The letter stated that a young partner, Balthasar, would take his place. (Balthasar was really Portia in disguise.) The Duke did not object to the change of lawyers. He did wonder though, if Balthasar was experienced enough to handle this trial. He looked at her carefully. He raised his eyebrows, but he said nothing. He could not recall seeing such a young lawyer in his courtroom. Since he respected Bellario, he instructed Balthasar to begin the trial.

Portia looked around the huge courtroom. Everyone was waiting for her to begin. She glanced at Shylock. He was grinning and seemed to be enjoying his day in court. Antonio looked very unhappy. He looked at her with begging eyes. Portia then looked over at her husband. Bassanio had no idea that the lawyer defending his friend was really his wife. He was pale with fear and sick from worry. Portia did not think he would even recognize his own mother today.

The room began to grow quiet. So quiet. Portia looked around one more time. This was truly an enormous task before her. Could she handle this? Many people faced with such a task would panic. Not Portia. The importance of the task ahead made her feel strong.

Too many people were counting on her. She could not let them down.

Portia walked down the aisle to the witness box. She spoke to Shylock, the first witness. Portia reminded Shylock that he had the right to the terms of the loan agreement. She did not argue that point. "Sir," she said, "the laws of Venice allow you the terms of your loan agreement. There is no question about that." Then she spoke to him of other choices he had. Of more noble choices. She reminded him the value of mercy. "You are in a position to show mercy to this man."

"Why should I show this scum mercy?" said Shylock with scorn.

Portia answered, "Mercy is like the gentle rain. It falls from heaven. It is blessed twice. The person who gives the mercy is blessed. The person who gets the mercy is also blessed." The courtroom grew quiet as Portia spoke. The people were impressed with this young attorney. Portia went on, "Sir, mercy is a more gorgeous crown than one that sparkles with gold and jewels. Justice with mercy is better than justice without mercy. You have the power to give Antonio his life. To do that you must show mercy."

All eyes in the courtroom were on Portia. The residents of Venice thought her speech rang true. All except Shylock. His only answer was to say that he wanted the terms of the loan agreement enforced. "I don't care about mercy. I care only for justice!" he screamed. "I want justice and I want it now!" He had great anger in his voice.

Portia was starting to get more nervous. She didn't want to show it though. She came back in a strong, steady voice, "Can Antonio pay you back now?"

Bassanio jumped up and quickly said, "I have offered to pay Shylock the three thousand ducats plus as much additional money as he wants. I offer it again now. As much money as you want for my friend. Any amount you name is yours."

Shylock refused, "You're wasting your breath. It's too late for repayment." He wanted only revenge.

Bassanio then begged Portia to try to change the law so that Antonio would be saved. "The law doesn't have to grant the terms of the agreement. There must be a way to get around the exact terms of the loan. The law can be applied in many different ways."

Portia answered, "Laws were not made to be altered. We must respect the law, not try to think of ways to get around it."

At this point, Portia asked to see the written loan agreement. She read to the quiet courtroom, "If the terms of this loan agreement are not kept, the money lender may lawfully claim a pound of flesh. The flesh is to be cut from a section of the body that is closest to Antonio's heart. The money lender is the person who will cut into the body and take the flesh." The courtroom was silent. It seemed as if all had stopped breathing.

"Shylock," said Portia in a hushed, pleading voice, "be merciful. Take the money and let me tear up the loan agreement."

Shylock grinned and said, "You will never change my mind. I will not allow the agreement to be changed. Not for any reason. And that is that."

"Antonio," said Portia in a matter of fact way, "you must prepare your chest for the knife." There was a gasp from those watching. People could not believe it. Shylock began sharpening his long knife. He looked as if he could not wait to cut into Antonio.

Portia once again turned to Antonio, "Have you anything to say before the deed?"

"I have nothing to say to the court except that I am

ready for death." Then he turned to Bassanio, "Good-bye. Do not blame yourself for my death. It is not your fault. Give my best regards to your wife. Tell her that you were the best friend anyone could ever have."

Bassanio was beside himself with grief. "Antonio," he said, "I am married to a wonderful woman who means as much as life itself to me. Yet I must tell you that my life, that of my wife, and all of the rest of the world do not mean more to me than you. I would give anything if I could save you right now. I would sell my soul and that of my loved ones to the devil for your life."

Portia was shocked to hear these words. She was not really insulted. She knew how upset Bassanio was at the thought of losing his friend. Still, she could not resist saying, "Bassanio, it is a good thing that your wife is not here right now. She would not like to hear these words. She would probably be upset that you offered to sacrifice her to the devil." Bassanio was too upset to hear her words.

Gratiano did hear them. He had been listening intently. He loved to copy everything Bassanio did. He made a similar speech about his wife. "I also have a wonderful wife whom I love dearly. Yet I, too, would gladly give her up if I thought it would change Shylock's mind."

As Portia's clerk, Nerissa had been quietly writing when she heard her husband's words. She looked up. She also felt called upon to answer. "Sir, it is a good thing your wife is not here either. I'm afraid your home would no longer enjoy peace if she heard your words."

At this point, Shylock cried out, "Oh, stop it, everyone. I'm tired of listening to this nonsense. Let's get on with it." With these heartless words, the crowd was once again quiet. The crowd's feelings were with Antonio. Women were softly sobbing. Men were shaking their heads in sad silence.

Portia asked the court, "Are the scales ready for weighing the pound of flesh?" The Duke slowly nodded. "Shylock," said Portia, "you must have a surgeon here so that Antonio will not bleed to death."

Shylock was stunned for a moment. He was not sure how to answer. Of course, it was his intent that Antonio should bleed to death. What was this lawyer getting at? He finally answered, "The loan agreement doesn't say anything about a doctor's being present."

Portia answered him, "That may be true, but you could still offer this as a matter of kindness."

"But the loan agreement says nothing of this," said Shylock again. He repeated this a third time. "Look here, the papers say nothing about having a doctor here."

"Very well," said Portia, "A pound of Antonio's flesh is yours. The law allows it. The court awards it. You may take this pound from his chest."

Shylock was thrilled that he was finally going to be allowed to kill Antonio. He never really thought the law would allow him to kill his enemy. He wanted to get even with Antonio for encouraging his daughter to leave home. Shylock felt that Antonio and Bassanio were to blame for the loss of both his daughter and his money. He had made himself sick with hatred. He could taste revenge.

Shylock couldn't resist telling Portia how pleased he was with her decision. "You are such a wise lawyer. You are an honorable attorney. What a just verdict." Then he said to Antonio as he sharpened his knife, "Come here. Let's get on with the verdict." He looked into Antonio's eyes, but he did not really see him. He saw only his daughter's face. The face he would never see again.

Portia interrupted, "Just a moment, Shylock. There is just one minor detail. This loan agreement does not give you one drop of blood. There is nothing in this agreement that says you may take any blood. If you shed just one drop of this man's blood, you will break the law. One drop of blood means that the City of Venice will take your land and all your goods. Do you understand?"

Shylock was speechless. The words started to sink in slowly. Things had changed. In an instant revenge had slipped out of his grasp. It would be impossible for him to take a pound of flesh without shedding a good deal of blood. He started to turn red with anger. The hush in the courtroom gave way to whispers. People were talking about the genius of this young lawyer. She had turned the tables on Shylock. She used his reasoning against him. This clever lawyer had used the terms of his agreement to save Antonio. There was no mention of blood in the loan papers. Shylock could not legally take any blood. Therefore, he could not get the flesh either.

The whispers in the courtroom gave way to applause. Everyone was relieved. Antonio was going to live. What a clever lawyer, they thought. Gratiano was the first to call out, "You are the wisest attorney. What an honorable man of law we have before us. What a just verdict!"

Shylock realized that he was beaten. He was bitterly disappointed. He started to think how he could still get something out of this. "If I can't have my pound of flesh, then I'll just take the money that is owed."

"Here it is. Take it right away," said Bassanio, who was thrilled. He was so grateful that he would not lose his friend. As he was handing the bag to Shylock, Portia stopped him.

"Not so fast," she said. "The money lender is not entitled to anything but the penalty. Shylock, you must prepare to take the flesh. Remember, do not take any blood. Not one drop. Also, do not take an ounce more or an ounce less than you are owed. If you do, there will be punishment. You will be condemned to die. Do you understand? You will die and all your wealth will be turned over to the state."

"Give me my money and let me go," said Shylock.

"Here it is," offered Bassanio. "Take it and get out of here." Shylock headed toward the money. Portia once again stopped him.

"Just a minute, Shylock. You can be arrested for yet another crime. According to the laws of Venice, you have plotted to kill a fellow Venetian. Your intent was to kill this man. By law, your wealth should be turned over to the state. Your life may also be taken for this crime. You are at the mercy of the Duke. Get down on your hands and knees. Beg for a pardon."

"Because I am a Christian," said the Duke, "I am going to pardon you. In the spirit of forgiveness, I give you your life. You do not have to beg for it. This is the Christian way. I must punish your deed though. For trying to kill this man, I command you to turn half of your wealth over to Antonio. The other half goes to the City of Venice."

Antonio was always a generous man. Even after what had happened, he did not change. He knew that Shylock had cut his daughter out of his will. He started to think of ways to help Jessica and her new husband. "If the court agrees," said Antonio, "I have a request about the money."

The Duke of Venice asked, "What is your request?" The courtroom became quiet again. The people leaned forward to hear.

"I will take only half of Shylock's money. The other half I want to go to his daughter. I have another request. I want Shylock to put his daughter back into his will. He has recently cut her out of his will because she married

33

against his wishes." Antonio was pleased that he had the chance to help this young couple. He knew that they were having money problems. After all, the money was rightfully hers. She was Shylock's only heir.

"That is a fair and just request. I rule that Shylock show proof of a new will giving his only child his money when he dies. If you do not do this," said the Duke to Shylock, "I will take my pardon back and you will face death."

Shylocks color had turned from red to a pale green. He had never felt so ill. The loss of the money and revenge was making him sick. "Let me go home. I am ill. I promise to send the will showing that my daughter will inherit my wealth. Please let me go now."

"Get out then," said the Duke. "Make sure you don't forget to change your will. You are free to go now, Antonio," said the Duke. He turned to Portia and praised her. "I have never had a chance to see such a brilliant legal mind," he said. "Young lawyer, you have impressed me today. Please come home with me and have dinner. I want to discuss law with you."

Portia was flattered by this invitation. But she wanted to get home before her husband. "I would love to come, but I have another case to attend. Thank you for your kind words." The duke was disappointed, yet he understood. A young lawyer with a mind this clever must be in high demand.

He turned to Antonio, "You should pay this lawyer well. I don't have to remind you how much you owe him. Do I?" He then left the courtroom.

Bassanio began talking to Portia, "Sir, my friend and I can never repay you, but please let us give you something. Please take the three thousand ducats."

Antonio joined in, "We must pay you. We insist. No matter how much you ask, it is not enough. We will still be in your debt. For our whole lives we will owe you."

Portia refused to take the money. "Thank you, but no thank you. It is not necessary to pay me."

The men did not understand her lack of interest in the money. It was frustrating to them. They pleaded with her to take money. Bassanio finally said, "Please, I have to ask you again. Take something. Take anything. Let us give you something."

Portia answered, "Antonio, if you must give me something, I will take your gloves. I could use a pair."

As Antonio was pulling off the gloves, Portia got an idea. She started to think of a good trick to play on her husband. She would get the ring from him as payment. Then she would scold him for coming home without it.

"Bassanio, I have changed my mind. You do have something I would like. I would like that ring." She pointed directly to his wedding ring. Bassanio was too surprised to answer right away.

He finally said, "I cannot give you this ring. It is a wedding gift from my wife. I promised her I would never ever part with it. But I will find you the most valuable ring in all of Venice. And I will buy that one for you."

Portia pretended that she was insulted. As she turned to leave the courtroom, she said, "I am not going to beg. It is clear that your generosity has its limits." She walked out of the courtroom. Nerissa followed.

Antonio could not stand it any longer. "Please, Bassanio, please give him the ring. I know your wife will be mad, but think about what this man has done for us today. We must repay him for my life. That must be more important than your wife's anger." Bassanio felt ashamed. It was true. This young lawyer had done them a service that could never be repaid.

He sent Gratiano after Portia with the ring. When the clerk, Nerissa, saw this, she asked Gratiano if he also had a ring. Of course, Gratiano wanted to be just like Bassanio, so he quickly gave his wedding ring to her. As soon as Portia and Nerissa were alone, they had a good laugh. They started planning for the evening when their husbands would both return without rings. Perhaps they should accuse Bassanio and Gratiano of giving their rings to another woman. What fun they would have as their husbands squirmed with guilt!

Portia was in a wonderful mood when she returned to her house. She had never felt so happy. The feeling that comes with a good deed is one of the best that life can offer. As she looked out at the moon, she felt it had never shined so brightly. When she heard music, she thought it sounded so much sweeter this evening. She and Nerissa had changed back into their own clothes. They began to await the arrival of their husbands.

# Part V

When the men arrived, they were warmly welcomed. But the greetings were scarcely over, when a quarrel started. Nerissa and Gratiano were having a heated argument in the corner of the room. "Whatever is the matter?" asked Portia. "Good gracious. The two of you have been together only minutes. What could you be fighting about already?"

"It is about a silly thing really. Nerissa gave me a ring that was inscribed *Love me, and leave me not.* It was worth practically nothing," said Gratiano.

"Worth nothing! How can you say that?" cried Nerissa. "You swore to me that you would keep that ring forever. Till the exact hour of your death. Now you tell me that you kept it only hours. You gave it to a lawyer's clerk. How could you? I know that you gave it to another woman." With this Nerissa started to cry.

Gratiano became upset. "I swear to you, I gave it to a boy. This boy was the clerk of the lawyer who saved Antonio's life. What could I do? He begged me for it."

Portia said, "Gratiano, you never should have given your wedding ring away. I don't care who asked you for it. I gave Bassanio a ring also. I am certain that he would never part with it. You should try to be more like your master."

"But he did! He did!" said Gratiano. "I never would have given Nerissa's ring away if Bassanio had not given up yours. I was just doing what he did. He set the example. I followed it."

When Portia heard this, she pretended to be furious. She waited to calm herself. Then she spoke, "Nerissa was right. Both of you men gave our sacred wedding rings to other women. How could you?" Bassanio was sick with guilt. He loved Portia so much. He couldn't stand the thought that she believed he was untrue to her.

"Oh, Portia, never would I do such a thing," he cried. "I gave it to a lawyer because he saved my best friend's life. What could I do? I did not want to be ungrateful for my friend's life. I did not want to give your ring away either. I think if you had been there, you would have made me give the ring to the lawyer."

"It's my fault," said Antonio. "I am causing all of these quarrels. I'm going to leave now so you can work out these problems. Forgive me for making you fight."

"No, Antonio, please don't go. It is not your fault," said Portia.

"Portia, it is my fault. I promise you that Bassanio will never again break his word to you. This was just a very strange thing that occurred. It will not happen again," vowed Antonio.

"Then you must be his conscience in the future. Give him this ring. Tell him to keep it forever. Or at least longer than he kept that last one!" said Portia. When Bassanio looked at the ring, he was puzzled. He could not believe that this was the same ring that he had given the lawyer. But it was. How did this happen?

Portia and Nerissa both started to giggle. Their giggles turned to hearty laughter. The men stood by with puzzled looks. Finally Portia began to tell their story. Bassanio could not believe that his wife was even more wonderful than he had thought. His wife was the most clever woman in all Italy. She was responsible for saving his best friend's life. He was overcome with joy and gratitude.

As if Portia's secret was not enough, there was still more to come. A messenger brought news that Antonio's ships had not been lost at sea. They had safely arrived in the harbor. The goods were ready for sale. There could not possibly have been a happier night for this group of friends. They celebrated late into the night under a beautiful Italian moon. They laughed again about the rings. They laughed some more about husbands who can't recognize their own wives.

As the evening wore on, Gratiano swore over and over that for as long as he lived, he would fear only one thing. Of course, that would be the safekeeping of his wife's ring!

# THE
# MERCHANT
# OF VENICE

## THE PLAY

# Cast of Characters

BASSANIO | friends
ANTONIO |
SHYLOCK, *a rich money lender*
PORTIA, *a wealthy heiress*
GRATIANO, *Bassanio's servant*
NERISSA, *Portia's maid*
JESSICA, *Shylock's daughter*
LORENZO, *Jessica's husband*
BALTHASAR, *Portia's servant*
DUKE OF VENICE, *officer of the Venetian court*
MUSICIAN
COURTROOM CROWD

# Part I

**Setting: A street in Venice.**

*(Antonio and Bassanio enter.)*

ANTONIO: How is everything going for you, my friend?

BASSANIO: I'm afraid I have a problem, Antonio. I was hoping that you might be able to help me.

ANTONIO: Tell me your problem. Haven't I always told you that *your* problems are *my* problems? Whatever I have is yours. All you need to do is ask.

BASSANIO: I will tell you what has been bothering me. I have met a woman and fallen in love. She is the most beautiful woman you could ever imagine. Her hair is the color of the sun. Her eyes are as blue as the sea. She is an angel. And she also happens to be rich.

ANTONIO: How fortunate for you. To meet a woman who is both beautiful and rich. You are a lucky dog!

BASSANIO: There is one problem.

ANTONIO: Perhaps she does not share your feelings?

BASSANIO: No, that's not it. In fact, every time our eyes meet, she gives me reason to believe that she loves me.

ANTONIO: Then what is the problem?

BASSANIO: She is so beautiful and rich that men from all

corners of the world are chasing her. How can I compete with them when I have no money? I need to shower her with gifts. Flowers, candy, jewelry. I can't just go to her home and say, "Look here, Portia" – that is her name – "I don't have any money. But you have plenty for both of us. Marry me so that I can live a life of luxury." Why would she choose me when she could have anyone?

ANTONIO: But if she loves you . . .

BASSANIO: I don't know that she loves me *that* much!

ANTONIO: I understand. I want to help you. But I also have a big problem. All of my money is tied up. I've got three ships filled with rich goods out at sea. When they dock, I'll have plenty of money. Right now I have nothing.

BASSANIO: I'm doomed. I'll never win the hand of this lady. It's all over.

ANTONIO: Not so fast, my friend. I think I know how we can solve your problem. I know a money lender who always has cash. His name is Shylock. We'll go to him and ask for a loan. He is certain to lend you the money if I sign the loan agreement.

BASSANIO: I can sign the agreement. You don't have to sign for me.

ANTONIO: He may not agree to those terms. He knows I have the means to back up a loan. As soon as my ships come in, we'll pay him back.

BASSANIO: That's great. Let's go find him now. I don't want to lose any time. Someone could be proposing to Portia as we speak.

*(Antonio and Bassanio exit.)*

**Setting: A room in Portia's house in Belmont.**

*(Portia and Nerissa, her servant, enter.)*

PORTIA: Nerissa, I have to tell you. I'm getting tired of this life.

NERISSA: You don't really have such a bad life. You're rich and beautiful. I should be so lucky.

PORTIA: If I were less rich, I might be in a better position. It is not fair that I have nothing to say about who I'm going to marry. I want to make the choice! I'm the person who is going to spend my whole life with the man. Why is it that my father made this decision? It is a great injustice. My dead father has a greater hold over my life than I do. How can this be?

NERISSA: Don't be so hard on your father. He was a very good man. Like every wise father, he was trying to do the best for his only daughter. But I agree with you. It seems that this idea about the three chests is not the best way to choose a husband. You must remember though, if your father thought it was a good idea, it will probably work. He must have thought carefully about the contest involving the gold, silver, and lead chests. Your father believed that the man who finds your picture inside would also be the wisest choice for your husband. You have to have faith in your father. Tell me, so far, do you like any of the suitors who have come?

PORTIA: Let's go through the list. You name them. I'll tell you what I think of them.

NERISSA: First, there's the Prince.

PORTIA: That man is a bore. He talks only of his horse. He's so proud that he can shoe his own horse. His whole conversation is about his horse. Do I look like his groomsman?

NERISSA: Then there is the Count.

PORTIA: He does nothing but frown. What a long, droopy face! Even when he's telling jokes, he looks as if he's describing a funeral. Can you imagine? If he's that sad when he's a young man, he'll be deeply depressed by the time he reaches old age. So you see, I have a great choice so far. I'd rather be married to a skull and crossbones than either of those two.

NERISSA: What about the Frenchman?

PORTIA: I know it's not nice to make fun of people, but I can't help myself. The Frenchman has a horse better than the Prince. He has a frown more frightening than the Count.

NERISSA: What do you say about the young Baron of England?

PORTIA: I don't say anything to him because he can't speak Italian. As a matter of fact, he can't speak Latin or French either. He knows only one language. And I'm not that good in English. He must be very ignorant to know only one language!

NERISSA: What do you think of the young German?

PORTIA: I don't like him when he's sober. And I like him less when he's drunk. Since he's usually drunk, I usually don't like him at all. I call him the sponge.

NERISSA: It's just as well that you don't like these men. They all ran home quickly when they learned of your father's terms for choosing a husband for you. They didn't mind the idea of choosing the right chest from three. That was all right. It was your father's penalty for choosing the wrong chest they didn't like. The promise to remain bachelors for the rest of their lives scared them off. It's one thing to lose a wife. It's another to lose the right to have any wife forever.

PORTIA: They each made the right decision. Good riddance.

NERISSA: Do you remember a man from Venice? He came here when your father was alive. This man was a scholar and a soldier.

PORTIA: Yes, of course, I remember him. How could I forget? His name was Bassanio.

NERISSA: I think that he was the best suitor that you have had so far.

PORTIA: You may be right. Let's not talk about him. It just makes me feel sad.

(A servant enters.)

SERVANT: Madam, the four visitors have all left now. A messenger for the Prince of Morocco has just arrived. The Prince will be here this evening.

PORTIA: I wish I could say I was happy about that. I'm not. At least I can say that I'm glad the others have gone. Come with me, Nerissa. Let's get ready for the latest bachelor who knocks on my door!

49

**Setting: A public place in Venice.**

*(Shylock is already there. Antonio and Bassanio enter.)*

ANTONIO: Shylock, I have a request for you. I would like you to lend my best friend three thousand ducats. I'll be glad to sign the loan papers with Bassanio. You can count on me to pay any interest you might ask.

BASSANIO: You can be sure that I'm good for this loan. I will pay you back. If you doubt that, Antonio's name on the loan should be enough for you.

SHYLOCK: Three thousand ducats and Antonio's signature?

BASSANIO: Yes, that's right. What is your answer?

SHYLOCK: Antonio is known to pay his debts.

BASSANIO: Is your answer 'yes'?

SHYLOCK: Now just a minute. I didn't say that. Antonio is well thought of in Venice. And I know that he now has three ships at sea. He has one coming from Africa. One comes from England. And I believe one comes from Mexico. That's a big risk. What if they don't make it? Pirates could rob the ships. Storms could sink them all. Nothing is certain. Still, I think I might make the loan.

BASSANIO: Let's go out to dinner. We'll talk more about this loan.

SHYLOCK: I never eat with Christians. I may walk with them, lend them money. But I refuse to eat with them. Not ever. I don't want to sit there and smell pork. It turns my stomach.

BASSANIO: Very well, then. Just give me the loan. What about it?

ANTONIO: Are you going to give us the money or not?

SHYLOCK: Antonio, do you recall all those times that you insulted me? Do you remember spitting on my clothes? And calling me a dog? Now you want to borrow money from a dog! Does a dog have money? Go find one with three thousand ducats. You have the nerve to ask me for a loan after insulting me.

ANTONIO: Let me tell you the truth. Even though I ask you for a loan, I haven't changed my mind about you. I still think you are a dog. I look forward to spitting on you again in the future. I'm not asking you for a favor. You are no friend of mine. Make no mistake about that. I'm asking you for a loan. Lend me the money as if I were your worst enemy. If I don't pay you back, you can place a heavy fine on me.

SHYLOCK: You don't have to be so angry all the time. I would like nothing better than to be friends with you. I am willing to let bygones be bygones. I will give you the loan. I'm not even going to charge you interest.

ANTONIO: What did you say?

SHYLOCK: I said you have misjudged me. I am not the heartless person that you think. You are in need of help. I am here to assist you. I'm going to give you the three thousand ducats interest free.

ANTONIO: Is it possible that I may have judged you too harshly?

SHYLOCK: I think you have. I am happy to lend you this money. I want only your respect and gratitude. I ask that you think about the way you have misjudged me in the past. Also, I would ask something else. Let me see. How could we seal this bargain? I have it!

ANTONIO: What? How can we seal this agreement?

SHYLOCK: I've got an idea. Come with me and see a lawyer. Sign an agreement that says there will be no interest for this loan. But if you don't pay it back, you will give me a pound of your flesh. From any part of your body that I choose! This will be a great joke that other merchants will talk about for years to come. Please come along. No one will ever believe this!

BASSANIO: A pound of flesh! That's not even funny.

ANTONIO: I will be happy to sign your loan agreement. I am touched by your kindness.

*(Bassanio pulls Antonio aside.)*

BASSANIO: Please don't sign any paper with those terms. I don't trust him.

ANTONIO: You're going to get your money, your fancy clothes, and your wife! This fellow just wants a good laugh. After all, it's only fair. I've made him feel bad many times. This is his way of forgiving and forgetting. Besides, my ships are as good as in the dock now. Quit worrying! Nothing can go wrong.

BASSANIO: I have a bad feeling about this deal.

SHYLOCK: You Christian fellows really are suspicious. Is that how your religion teaches you to live? Listen here. What could I possibly have to gain by taking a pound of flesh from your friend? What would I do with such a thing? A pound of beef or a pound of lamb would be another thing. There is no risk to this loan agreement. An interest-free loan and a bond of friendship. I don't know what more that I could do. Perhaps I'll just say good-bye. I wish you better luck with another money lender.

*(Shylock starts to exit.)*

ANTONIO: Wait! My friend is too careful. He's like an old lady. I'll sign your loan papers. I thank you for this chance. I understand that my signature means – as you say it does – that we are friends who must trust one another. Let's get on with the closing so my friend can get on with his life!

*(Shylock, Antonio, and Bassanio exit.)*

# Part II

**Setting: A street in Venice.**

*(Lorenzo and Jessica enter.)*

LORENZO: Jessica, we must make plans to be married. We will have to elope. Your father will never give consent.

JESSICA: That is true. He is such an angry man. He will never listen to reason. If I were to tell him that I had fallen in love with a Christian, he would be outraged. He would never allow us to meet again.

LORENZO: I have to get you back to your home before he discovers you are gone.

JESSICA: I hate to leave you. My home is a sad one. I can never remember any happiness there. Not since my mother died when I was a little girl. My father is never there. When he comes home, he spends all of his time counting money. What a sorry life that is. At least I can look forward to being with you soon. I'll be happy when the day comes that I never have to go back to that house.

LORENZO: It will be soon, my love. I am working very hard so that we can have a place of our own when we marry. Until that time I will continue to live with Bassanio. I have to save

55

money for us to start our new life.

JESSICA: Won't it be wonderful when we have our own place? A house for the two of us.

LORENZO: But soon there will be more.

JESSICA: What a happy thought! Our house will ring with laughter and love. I've been thinking. It might be better if I converted to your religion since we will be husband and wife.

LORENZO: Oh, Jessica, I would be so happy if you would!

JESSICA: I will always be Jewish in my heart. But I think it will be better for our family if we have the same religion.

LORENZO: I'm very happy that you would do this for me and our children. I want to talk with you more about it. But now we must go. Your father will be very upset if he doesn't find you when he arrives.

*(Lorenzo and Jessica exit.)*

# Part III

**Setting: A room in Portia's house. Three chests sit side by side.**

*(Enter Bassanio, Portia, Gratiano, and Nerissa.)*

PORTIA: Bassanio, I am glad you have come today.

BASSANIO: Your words are music to my ears. There isn't any other place I would rather be than here with you.

PORTIA: Don't choose the box today. Wait a few days. Please.

BASSANIO: Why should I wait? The sooner I choose, the sooner you will be my wife.

PORTIA: What if you choose the wrong box? I will lose you forever.

BASSANIO: I must choose now. This is like torture to me. I have to find out now if I can be your husband.

PORTIA: Please, I beg of you. Say that you will stay here with me for a few days. No, stay a month. I will teach you how to choose the right chest. What am I saying? I can't do that. I promised my father.

BASSANIO: I must choose now. I can't wait a minute longer.

PORTIA: If you must, you must. First let me get a musician to play for you while you are choosing. This might help.

*(Musician enters and begins to play.)*

*(Bassanio walks over to the golden chest.)*

BASSANIO: This is not it. It is too obvious. Everyone would choose the gold on first thought. Not I. Portia's father was trying to separate good men from fools.

*(Bassanio moves to the silver chest.)*

This is not it either. It would be the second most likely choice.

*(Bassanio moves to the lead chest.)*

This is it! I feel it in my bones.

*(Bassanio opens the chest slowly and takes out Portia's tiny portrait and a scroll.)*

I will read the words of Portia's father:

> *You that are so good and true*
> *Found that fortune fell to you*
> *Be content and seek no new.*
> *If you are well pleased with this*
> *Turn to where your lady is*
> *And claim her with a loving kiss.*

*(Bassanio turns to Portia.)*

I'm so happy. I can't find the words to tell you of my joy.

*(Bassanio runs to Portia. He kisses her and then holds her in his trembling arms.)*

PORTIA: I can't believe this. I am the luckiest woman in all of Italy. No, in the whole world!

BASSANIO: My dear Portia, I am not worthy of you. You

are like a goddess sitting far above me.

PORTIA: Please do not say anymore. You are making me feel bad. If I had one wish, I wish that I could be more beautiful for you. If I could be a thousand times more beautiful, then maybe I would deserve you. No, I would have to be a thousand times more beautiful and ten thousand times richer.

BASSANIO: Please! It is *I* who do not deserve *you*.

PORTIA: Take this ring. Show me that you will accept me and all I have. Promise me that you will never take it off. If you part with this ring, then you no longer love me.

BASSANIO: I have no more words to tell you of my love. I can promise you if I part with your ring, it is because I am dead. There could be no other reason.

GRATIANO: Excuse me, sir. Could I interrupt?

BASSANIO: Yes, what is it?

GRATIANO: Let me be the first to congratulate you and Portia. Now, I have a request for you. Would it be possible that I could also marry?

BASSANIO: I would love to see you get married. I want you to be as happy as I am right now. But how could you find someone to marry you? I don't mean to say that. I meant to say I only hope that you can find someone you truly love to be your wife.

GRATIANO: Sir, I have already found one. I love her dearly. She returns my love. We have waited a long time to ask you. Our love rested on your luck with the chests.

BASSANIO: What do you mean?

GRATIANO: Nerissa and I have been in love for some time. We did not think that it would be wise to say anything until after the outcome of the contest. You can imagine how happy we were when you chose the right chest.

PORTIA: Is this true, Nerissa?

NERISSA: Yes, it is true. But you know I would marry only if you approve.

BASSANIO: Your marriage is the best possible thing that could happen. We would be honored to have you married at our own wedding. It will be a double wedding. This calls for a celebration!

*(A servant enters. He gives Bassanio a letter.)*

SERVANT: This message is for you. Lord Bassanio.

*(Bassanio sits down and reads.)*

PORTIA: What on earth is the matter?

BASSANIO: You will never believe this. This is the worst thing that could ever have happened.

PORTIA: What is it? Please tell me!

BASSANIO: This is my fault. I haven't been completely honest with you. I told you that I was broke. I didn't tell you I was also in debt. I had to ask my best friend for the money to bring you gifts. My friend had to borrow money from a lender for me. The penalty for failing to repay the loan was a pound of flesh from my friend's body. Nobody took the penalty seriously. We thought we would pay back the loan without any problem. Now listen to the words of my friend's letter.

*Dear Bassanio,*

*My ships are all lost. The unthinkable has happened. Shylock has insisted that the penalty be enforced. Everyone has tried to talk him out of this. Even the Duke of Venice has tried. He will listen to no one. He is really going to take a pound of my flesh. I am going to die. Please come to the trial and to my execution. It has been set for two days from now. I want to see you one more time before I die. I will understand if you do not come. It is going to be a gruesome event.*

*Your friend, Antonio*

PORTIA: Go to your friend at once. I will give you enough money to repay this debt. I will give you twenty times the original sum. Go at once before your friend is harmed. You will never forgive yourself unless you save him.

BASSANIO: Thank you for understanding. I will leave now.

PORTIA: No, wait. Before you go, we should be married. If you are my husband, you will legally have the right to all my money. You must use whatever you need to save Antonio. Let's call for a priest.

*(Portia and Bassanio exit.)*

**Setting: (later) A room in Portia's house.**

*(Portia and her servant, Balthasar, enter.)*

PORTIA: Do you remember my cousin Bellario? He is the lawyer who lives in Padua. You must go quickly to his house. Give him this letter.

Wait for his answer. Bring back his answer
and the clothes he will give you. These will be
the robes that a lawyer wears to court. Do
you understand?

BALTHASAR: I will go now. I will return as soon as
possible.

*(Balthasar exits. Nerissa enters.)*

PORTIA: Nerissa, come with me. We must pack our
bags. We are on our way to Venice.

NERISSA: Are we going to see our husbands?

PORTIA: Yes, we are going to see them. But they will
not see us.

NERISSA: I don't understand.

PORTIA: You will soon know the meaning of my words.

*(Portia and Nerissa exit.)*

# Part IV

**Setting: A courtroom in Venice.**

*(The Duke of Venice, Bassanio, Antonio, and the people of the court enter.)*

THE DUKE OF VENICE: I will have to dismiss this court today with a guilty verdict unless Antonio's attorney arrives soon. I am very sorry for you, Antonio. But there is nothing that I can do for you. You signed the loan agreement.

ANTONIO: I understand, your honor. I'm afraid all is lost.

*(Portia and Nerissa, wearing the disguises of an attorney and clerk, enter the courtroom.)*

NERISSA: If it please the court, I have an important letter from Antonio's lawyer, Bellario.

DUKE: I will read his letter.

*Your honor, I am very sorry. I will not be able to defend my client in court today. I am quite ill. I send in my place a very distinguished young lawyer. His name is Balthasar. Do not worry about his youth. He is wise beyond his years. I have given him careful instructions about my client's case. Please let the trial proceed.*

PORTIA: Your honor, I know everything about this case.

DUKE: Are you ready to begin your defense?

PORTIA: Yes, your honor. I would like to call Shylock as my first witness.

SHYLOCK: Nothing that you're going to say will change my mind or the law.

PORTIA: Very well, sir. The law of Venice allows you the terms of your loan agreement. There is no question about that. But you have choices in this matter. You are in a position to show mercy to this man.

SHYLOCK: Why should I show mercy to this scum?

PORTIA: Mercy is like the gentle rain. It falls from the heavens. It is twice blessed. The person who gives the mercy is blessed. The person who receives the mercy is also blessed. Mercy is a more gorgeous crown than one that sparkles with gold and jewels. Justice with mercy is much better than justice without mercy. You have the power to give Antonio his life. But to do that you must show mercy.

SHYLOCK: I don't care about mercy. I care only for justice! I want justice and I want it now!

PORTIA: Can Antonio pay you back?

BASSANIO: I have offered to pay him the three thousand ducats plus as much extra money as he wants. I offer it again now. As much money as you want for my friend. Any amount you name is yours.

SHYLOCK: You're wasting your breath. It's too late for repayment now.

BASSANIO: Please, young lawyer, find a way to get my friend out of this. The law doesn't have to grant Shylock the terms of the agreement. There must be a way to get around the terms of the loan. The law can be used in many different ways.

PORTIA: Laws are not made to be tampered with. To do so would be to make a joke of the law. That is not what lawyers were trained to do. We must respect the law, not try to work around it.

SHYLOCK: You are a wise lawyer. You may look young, but your wisdom is that of a much older person. I applaud your change of heart.

PORTIA: Let me read the terms of the agreement to the court. It says, "If the terms of this loan agreement are not kept, the money lender may lawfully claim a pound of flesh. The flesh is to be cut from a section of the body that is closest to Antonio's heart. The money lender is the person who will cut into the body and take the flesh." Sir, be merciful. Take the money. Let me tear up the loan agreement.

*(Shylock pulls a knife from his clothing and begins to sharpen it.)*

SHYLOCK: You will never change my mind. I will not allow the loan agreement to be changed. Not for any reason. And that is that.

PORTIA: Antonio, you must prepare your chest for the knife. Have you anything to say before the deed?

ANTONIO: I have nothing to say to the court. I am ready for death. *(He turns to Bassanio.)* Good-bye. Do not blame yourself for my death. It is not your fault. Give my best regards to your wife. Tell her that you were the best friend that anyone could ever have.

BASSANIO: Antonio, I am married to a wonderful woman who means as much as life itself to me. Yet, I must tell you that my life, the life of my wife, and all the rest of the world do not mean more to me than you. I would give anything if I could save you. I would sell my soul and that of my loved ones to the devil for your life.

PORTIA: Bassanio, it is a good thing that your wife is not here right now. She would not like to hear these words. She would probably be very upset that you offered to sacrifice her to the devil for the sake of your friend.

*(Laughter is heard from the courtroom audience.)*

GRATIANO: I also have a wonderful wife whom I love dearly, but I, too, would gladly give up her life if I thought it would change Shylock's mind.

NERISSA: Sir, it is a good thing that your wife is not here either. I'm afraid your house would no longer enjoy peace if your wife heard those words.

*(More laughter is heard in the courtroom.)*

SHYLOCK: Oh, stop it, everyone. I'm tired of listening to this. Let's get on with it.

*(Now soft crying is heard from the courtroom audience.)*

PORTIA: Are the scales ready for weighing the pound of flesh? *(The Duke of Venice nods his head.)*

Shylock, you must have a surgeon here so that Antonio will not bleed to death.

SHYLOCK: The loan agreement doesn't say anything about a doctor's being present.

PORTIA: That may be true, but you could still offer this as a matter of kindness.

SHYLOCK: But the loan agreement says nothing of this. *(He waves the papers at Portia.)* Look here, the papers say nothing about having a doctor present.

PORTIA: Very well. A pound of Antonio's flesh is yours. The law allows it. The court awards it. You may take this pound from his chest.

SHYLOCK: You are a wise lawyer. What an honorable attorney you are. *(He shakes his knife at Antonio.)* Let's get on with the judgment.

PORTIA: Just a moment, Shylock. There is just one minor detail. This loan arrangement does not give you one drop of blood. If you shed just one drop of this man's blood, you will be in big trouble. One drop of blood means that your land and all your goods will be taken by the City of Venice. Do you understand?

GRATIANO: You are the wisest attorney. What an honorable man of law we have before us. Now this is a just verdict!

SHYLOCK: What do you mean?

PORTIA: One drop of blood and all your land and goods will be taken by the City of Venice. Do you understand?

SHYLOCK: If I can't have my pound of flesh, then I'll just take the money that is owed to me.

BASSANIO: Here it is. Take it right away.

PORTIA: Not so fast. The money lender is not entitled to anything but the penalty. Shylock, you must prepare to take the flesh. Remember, do not take any blood. Not one drop. Also, do not cut off one ounce more or less than you are entitled. If you do, there will be punishment. You will be condemned to die. Do you understand? You will die and all your wealth will be turned over to the state.

SHYLOCK: Give me my money and let me go.

BASSANIO: Here it is. Take it and get out of here.

PORTIA: Just a minute. You can be arrested for yet another crime. According to the laws of Venice, you intended to kill this man. By law, your wealth should be turned over to the state. Your life may also be taken for this crime. You are at the mercy of the Duke. Get down on your knees. Beg for a pardon.

DUKE: I am going to pardon you. In the spirit of forgiveness, I give you your life. You do not have to ask for it. This is the Christian way. I must punish your deed though. For trying to kill this man, I command you to give half of your wealth to Antonio. The other half goes to the City of Venice.

ANTONIO: Your honor, if the court agrees, I have a request for the money.

DUKE: What is your request?

ANTONIO: I will take only half of the money. The other half I want to go to Shylock's daughter. I have another request. I want Shylock to put his daughter, Jessica, back into his will. He recently cut her out of his will because she married against his wishes.

DUKE: This is a fair and just request. I rule that Shylock bring me proof of a new will. It will give his only daughter his money when he dies. If he does not do this, I will take my pardon back, and he will face death.

SHYLOCK: Let me go home. I am ill. I promise to send the will showing that my daughter will inherit my wealth. Please let me go now.

DUKE: Get out then. Make sure you don't forget to change your will. *(The Duke turns to Antonio as Shylock leaves the courtroom.)* You are free to go now, Antonio. *(Then the Duke turns to Portia.)* I have never before seen such a brilliant legal mind. Young lawyer, you have really impressed me here today. Please come home with me and have dinner. I would like to discuss law with you.

PORTIA: I would like to come. But I have another case I must attend. I thank you for your kind words.

DUKE: *(to Antonio)* You should pay this lawyer well. I don't have to remind you how much you owe him, do I?

*(The Duke exits.)*

BASSANIO: Sir, my friend and I can never repay you. Please let us give you something. Take the three thousand ducats.

ANTONIO: We must pay you. We insist. No matter how much you ask, it is not enough. We will still be indebted to you. For our whole lives we will owe you.

PORTIA: Thank you, but no thank you. It is not necessary to pay me. A person can be paid in many ways. Consider me paid. I am so pleased with the verdict of this case.

BASSANIO: Please, I have to ask you again. Take something. Take anything. Let us give you something.

PORTIA: Antonio, if you must give me something, I will take your gloves. I could use a pair. Bassanio, as for you, I will take your ring.

BASSANIO: This ring? You want this ring? It is not good enough for you. It's a cheap trinket.

PORTIA: I want it. I will have nothing else.

BASSANIO: I cannot give you this ring. It is a wedding gift from my wife. I promised her that I would never part with it. I will find you the most valuable ring in all of Venice. I will buy it for you.

PORTIA: I am not going to beg. It is clear that your generosity has limits.

*(Portia and Nerissa exit.)*

ANTONIO: Please give him the ring. I know your wife will be angry. But think what this man has done for us today. We must repay him for my life. That must be more important than your wife's anger.

BASSANIO: Gratiano, take this ring and give it to the lawyer. Hurry. Go quickly while you can still catch him.

*(Gratiano exits. Antonio and Bassanio exit. Gratiano, Portia, and Nerissa enter.)*

GRATIANO: Sir, please wait. My lord has asked that I find

70

you and give you this ring.

PORTIA: Tell him that I thank him. I am very pleased to have this ring.

NERISSA: *(She turns to Portia.)* Let's see if I can get my husband's ring.

PORTIA: *(She turns to Nerissa.)* What a good idea. We could really tease our husbands.

NERISSA: Gratiano, if you are as gallant as your lord, you might give up your ring also. I would dearly like to have it as a remembrance of my hard work for this case. What do you say to that?

GRATIANO: This is a very important ring. It is my wedding ring. I vowed to my wife that I would never part with it.

NERISSA: I see. I guess I have my answer. You are not like your master. He is much more the gentleman than you are. It is a pity you can't be more like him.

GRATIANO: That is not true. He and I are the same. I follow very closely in his footsteps. To prove it, I will give you my ring. If my master can part with his wedding ring, so can I. We are cut from the same cloth.

NERISSA: That's the spirit. Your act of kindness is accepted. Good-bye.

71

# Part V

**Setting: Avenue outside Portia's house.**

*(Portia and Nerissa enter.)*

PORTIA: I can hardly wait for Bassanio to return.

NERISSA: I feel the same way. I am eager to see Gratiano.

*(Enter Bassanio, Antonio, and Gratiano. Nerissa and Gratiano move to the side.)*

PORTIA: Welcome home, my dear husband. I am so happy to see you.

BASSANIO: Not as happy as I am to see you. Please meet my friend Antonio and welcome him also.

PORTIA: I am pleased to meet you, sir. Welcome to our home.

GRATIANO: *(To Nerissa)* That's not true, Nerissa. You have me all wrong. I would never do such a thing.

PORTIA: A quarrel so soon? What is the matter? Good gracious. The two of you have been together only minutes. What could you be fighting about already?

GRATIANO: It is about a silly thing really. Nerissa gave me a ring that was inscribed "Love me and leave me not." It was worth little or nothing.

NERISSA: Worth nothing! How can you say that? You

swore to me that you would keep that ring forever. Till the exact hour of your death. Now you tell me that you kept it only hours. You gave it to a lawyer's clerk? Did you think I would believe that story? I know that you gave it to another woman. How could you? *(Nerissa begins to weep loudly.)*

GRATIANO: I swear to you, I gave to to a boy. This boy was the clerk of the lawyer who saved Antonio's life. What could I do? He begged me for it.

PORTIA: Gratiano, you never should have given your wedding ring away. I don't care who asked you for it. It was your wife's first gift. I also gave Bassanio a ring and made him swear never to part with it. Here he stands with the ring on his finger. If he gave it away, I would be furious. I am certain that he never would part with it. You should try to be more like your master.

GRATIANO: My lord gave his ring away. He did! I never would have given Nerissa's ring away if he had not given up yours. I was just doing what he did. He set the example. I followed it.

PORTIA: What? Bassanio, tell me this is not true. I cannot believe this.

BASSANIO: I wish I could lie and tell you it was not true. But I can't because you would know. Look at my finger. The ring is gone.

PORTIA: Nerissa was right to be angry. Both of you men gave our sacred wedding rings to other women. How could you?

BASSANIO: I would never do such a thing. I gave it to a

74

lawyer because he saved my best friend's life. What could I do? I did not want to be ungrateful for my friend's life. I did not want to give your ring away either. If you had been there with me, I think you would have made me give the ring to the lawyer.

ANTONIO: Please stop arguing. It's all my fault. I am causing all of these quarrels. I am going to leave now so you can work out these problems. Please forgive me for making you fight.

PORTIA: Antonio, please don't go. It is not your fault.

ANTONIO: It is my fault. I promise you that Bassanio will never again break his word to you. This was just a very strange thing that occurred. It will never happen again.

PORTIA: Then you must be his conscience in the future. Give him this ring. Tell him to keep it forever. Or at least longer than he kept the last one. *(Portia gives the ring to Antonio. Antonio gives the ring to Bassanio. Portia and Nerissa start to giggle.)* Bassanio, don't you see? I was the lawyer.

NERISSA: And I was his clerk.

BASSANIO: *(Turning to Gratiano.)* And we did not know our own wives! How can this be?

ANTONIO: If this is so, then it is you, Portia, to whom I owe my life. This beautiful and brilliant woman saved my life. Thank you more than I can say.

PORTIA: I have other news for you, Antonio. A messenger brought word that all of your ships have arrived in port. None was lost. All the goods are there.

ANTONIO: What a wonderful night this is. Let's celebrate!

GRATIANO: Let's have a party that lasts all night. We have many things to talk and laugh about. I have learned a thing or two tonight that I will never forget. For the rest of my life I will fear only one thing. That is, of course, the safekeeping of my wife's ring!

*(Everyone cheers.)*

# THE GLOBE THEATER

The Globe Theater may well be the most famous theater in the world, for it was here that Shakespeare and other literary giants of his day produced their plays and other dramatic works.

Shakespeare and several other well-known actors needed a place to perform and so they pooled their funds and designed and built the Globe in 1599. Since they were theatrical professionals in every sense of the word, the building fit their needs perfectly. The Globe was octagonally-shaped with a roofless inner pit into which the stage projected. Three galleries (balconies) rose one above the other, the topmost of which had a thatched roof. One day, in order to provide reality in a production of Shakespeare's *King Henry the Eighth*, a cannon was discharged. Unfortunately, this piece of stagecraft set fire to the thatched roof, and the entire building burned. It was rebuilt the following year but was torn down by the Puritans 30 years later who needed the space for houses.

Today in London work is underway to build a new Globe Theater using only materials that would have been found in the original Globe – a perfect setting to enjoy Shakespeare's genius.

# About the Editors

Peggy L. Anderson, PhD, is a professor and Special Education Program Coordinator at Metropolitan State College of Denver. She has taught students with learning disabilities at the elementary and middle school levels in South Carolina and Florida. Her master's degree is from the Citadel and her doctorate is from the University of Denver. She completed her postdoctoral work with the Department of Pediatrics at Johns Hopkins University. Her research interests have focused on language-learning disabilities, dyslexia, and inclusion issues.

Judith D. Anderson, JD, is a trial attorney in southern California, specializing in the defense of school districts. She has taught Shakespeare to high school students in the United States and the United Kingdom for ten years. As a Fullbright Scholar, she travelled extensively in the British Isles, and met with the Queen Mother of England. She received her bachelor's degree at Flagler College and her law degree at Southwestern University School of Law.